Starting a Digital Marketing Agency

A Comprehensive Guide for Entrepreneurs

Table of Contents

Chapter 1. Introduction

Dive into the dynamic world of digital marketing and discover your entrepreneurial potential with our special report, "Starting a Digital Marketing Agency: A Comprehensive Guide for Entrepreneurs." This resource is teeming with insights and practical strategies to help you navigate the outset of your digital marketing venture. It's not just about basic setups or bookish knowledge. Instead, the essence of this exclusive report lies in its action-oriented approach, honed by real-world cases, expert opinions, and proven tactics in the digital marketing landscape. Whether you're a seasoned entrepreneur ready to expand into digital marketing or a zealous newbie with a vision, this report is designed to boost your confidence, spark your creative thought process, and guide you to establish a thriving agency. Get set to embark on a thrilling journey, because a fulfilling digital marketing career awaits right around the corner.

Chapter 2. Determining Your Niche in Digital Marketing

Before embarking upon your entrepreneurial journey into the world of digital marketing, it is vital to identify and understand your niche. Your niche is your area of expertise or specialization, which will dictate the kind of services you offer, the clients you cater to, and how you position yourself against competitors. Determining your niche sets the stage for creating a sustainable and successful business model. Please see the following sections for a comprehensive guide to determining your niche in digital marketing.

2.1. Assessing Your Strengths and Skills

The first step in finding your niche begins with an introspection of your strengths, skills, and experience. Make a list of your abilities, professional expertise, and areas where your passion meets talent. This could include skills in social media marketing, SEO expertise, email marketing, or content creation among others. It's important to step into an area where you have a solid understanding or where you're ready to learn and improve. A thorough understanding of your strengths and weaknesses will guide your decision-making.

2.2. Identifying Industry Trends and Opportunities

After identifying your strengths, the next step is to understand the digital marketing landscape. It's critical that you stay updated with industry trends and emerging opportunities.

Conduct research by reading digital marketing reports, attending webinars and conferences, talking to industry leaders and experts, or following credible digital marketing blogs. Look for gaps in the market, untapped opportunities, or under-served areas where you can apply your strengths. Research can reveal developing markets, technological advancements, or new client types that may be ideal for your agency.

2.3. Understanding Customer Needs

Understand your potential customers and what they want. This aids in shaping your services and overall business strategy to meet client needs.

Create client personas by identifying their demographics, online behavior, preferences, pain-points, and digital marketing needs. Use surveys, focus groups, or online tools to gather data about your target audience. The better you understand your potential customers, the more value you can deliver through your digital marketing services.

2.4. Comparing Competitors

Every thriving industry has competition and digital marketing is no exception. Understanding your competition is crucial to form your niche and position your agency.

Identify competitors who offer similar services. Analyze their strengths, weaknesses, strategies, and unique selling points. Competitive analysis provides insights into the market standards, gaps in services, or unique approaches you can adopt to stand out.

2.5. Choosing a Profitable Niche

After thorough analysis and introspection, choose a niche. Consider your strengths, industry trends, customer needs, and competitive landscape.

Your chosen digital marketing niche should not only cater to your strengths and interests but also be profitable and sustainable. It can be tempting to dive into an emerging trend, but ensure it has the potential for long-term profitability.

Your niche could be a specific service, such as content marketing, a particular industry like real estate, or it could be a specific demographic, like small businesses. As you gain experience and understand the market better, you can even specialize in a combination of these niches.

2.6. Positioning Your Agency

Once you've chosen a niche, it's time to strategically position your agency in the market.

Your positioning strategy should focus on the unique value you offer to your target clients. Craft a compelling value proposition that highlights your distinctiveness and specializing in your niche. Position your agency as the go-to choice for your particular service.

2.7. Re-Evaluating Your Niche

Finding your niche is not a one-time task. As the digital marketing landscape evolves, your niche should evolve too. Keep abreast of industry trends, revisit your strengths, understand changing customer needs, watch for new competitors, and reassess your chosen niche's profitability.

In conclusion, determining your niche is an ongoing, cyclical process that requires constant research, self-evaluation, and flexibility. It's an integral part of starting a digital marketing agency, and therefore, must be approached with due diligence. With thoughtful planning and strategic decisions, you can find a niche that drives your agency towards lucrative success.

Chapter 3. Crafting an Effective Business Plan

A successful digital marketing agency starts from a well-crafted business plan. This indispensable document acts as your guiding star, directing your actions, investments, and aspirations in the right direction. It details your agency's vision, mission, target market, competitors, unique selling proposition (USP), and much more. Here, we will delicately unpack the process of crafting an effective business plan for your digital marketing agency.

3.1. Define Your Vision and Mission

The vision and mission statements of your agency provide direction and induce purpose in your business endeavours. A vision statement lays out the long-term goals of your agency, whereas your mission statement sets out what you aim to achieve in the immediate future.

1. **Vision Statement:** Start with scribbling down what you envision your agency to be in the future. Craft a statement that's impressive yet realistic. As a digital marketing agency, your vision could be to become a leader in providing innovative, customer-centric, and results-driven marketing solutions.

2. **Mission Statement:** Your mission statement should focus on present goals. It could be something as simple as helping businesses amplify their online presence, drive traffic, and increase conversions through expert digital marketing.

3.2. Identify Your Target Market

Understanding your target market is critical for the success of your agency. Knowing who your clients will be helps you refine your services, tailor your outreach, and cater specifically to their needs.

1. **Market Segmentation:** Segment your target market based on factors like industry type, business size, location, and specific needs.

2. **Market Analysis:** Analyze your target markets for their potential and challenges. This involves studying the market size, growth potential, and the competition.

3.3. Analyze Your Competitors

Analyzing your competition helps you uncover their strengths and weaknesses, which can be useful in designing your agency's unique value proposition.

1. **Competitor Profiling:** Create profiles for your main competitors detailing their strengths, weaknesses, offerings, and strategies.

2. **SWOT Analysis:** Conduct a SWOT analysis for each competitor, focusing on their Strengths, Weaknesses, Opportunities, and Threats.

3.4. Define Your Unique Selling Proposition (USP)

A USP is a unique benefit or advantage that you offer, differentiating you from your competitors. Your USP could lie in your cutting-edge technology, specialized industry knowledge, or a novel approach to digital marketing.

1. **Find Your Uniqueness:** Identify what sets you apart from your competitors and what you do better. This could be your comprehensive range of services, affordable pricing, or creative campaigns.

2. **Craft Your USP:** Combine the unique features and benefits into a compelling statement that attracts your target audience.

3.5. Set Your Financial Goals

Financial planning is a major part of your business plan. It includes revenue projection, cost estimation, pricing strategies and potential profitability.

1. **Revenue Projection:** Make an approximate estimate of your revenues for the first few years based on your market analysis and pricing strategy.

2. **Cost Estimation:** Calculate the costs of operations, marketing, and administration over the same period.

3. **Profitability Analysis:** Evaluate the profitability using the projected revenue and costs.

3.6. Develop Marketing and Sales Strategies

Defining the marketing and sales strategies involve deciding how you will attract and convert your potential clients.

1. **Marketing Strategy:** Decide on your marketing channels, the type of content you'll share, how you'll engage with your audience, and how you'll measure success.

2. **Sales Strategy:** Define your sales process, including lead generation, nurturing, conversion, and follow-up.

3.7. Prepare Your Operations Plan

The operations plan should outline how your agency will run on a daily basis. This includes the organizational structure, roles and responsibilities, processes, and resources.

1. **Organizational Structure:** Decide on the hierarchy of your team,

specifying the different roles and their respective responsibilities.

2. **Business Processes:** Outline the various processes in your agency, from invoicing clients to deploying digital marketing campaigns.

3.8. Risk Assessment and Mitigation

Understanding the risks involved in your business and devising strategies to mitigate them is essential for survival and growth.

1. **Risk Identification:** Identify potential risks, both internal and external, that might hamper operations or financial stability.

2. **Risk Mitigation Strategies:** Develop strategies to manage these risks, such as diversifying client base, constant learning and upgradation, etc.

Creating a compelling and effective business plan calls for meticulous research, clear vision, and careful execution. This document not only helps you in attracting investors and lenders, but it also enables you to keep your business on track and focused. Always remember, your business plan is dynamic and should evolve with your agency, requiring regular updates and alterations as you grow.

Chapter 4. Marquees of a Robust Digital Marketing Strategy

Defining a robust digital marketing strategy is crucial for any startup, as it helps establish the groundwork for success and leads toward attaining goals. The approach is the deciding factor that can make or break your digital marketing agency, so it should ideally be comprehensive, actionable, and adaptable.

4.1. Understanding Your Target Audience

Before anything else, understanding who you are marketing to is essential. Your target audience fuels and guides all your strategies, hence it's crucial to know them in depth.

Create user personas representing your ideal customers, with factors such as demographics, preferences, online behavior, and pain points. Utilize methods like interviews, surveys, studying competitor customers, and analyzing online data.

Remember, these personas are not static and need updating regularly as user behavior changes.

```
|===
|User Persona |Demographics |Preferences |Online
Behaviour |Pain Points

|Manager Mike
|35-45 years, Male, Based in New York, Income over $80K
|High-quality solutions, Quick responses
```

```
|Frequently online on LinkedIn, Twitter
|Too many tasks, not enough time

|Entrepreneur Emily
|25-35 years, Female, Based in Seattle, Income over $60K
|Innovation, Value for money
|Active Instagram, Facebook user
|Lack of reliable and affordable services
|===
```

4.2. Developing the Right Content Strategy

Quality content is the backbone of any digital marketing strategy. Improve brand visibility, drive traffic, and gain leads using thoughtfully crafted content.

Types of content can include blogs, ebooks, video content, infographics, webinars, podcasts, and more. Choose your content mix based on audience preferences to maximize resonance and engagement.

4.3. Social Media Marketing

Social media is a powerful means to reach your target audience. As a digital marketing agency, harness this potential by mastering each platform's nuances to engage better with your audience.

Facebook, LinkedIn, Twitter, and Instagram all have different user behaviors and content expectations. Know these differences, and tailor your content accordingly.

4.4. Search Engine Optimization

SEO is indispensable when it comes to ranking higher on search engine results. A proper SEO strategy will attract more organic traffic to your website, improving visibility and credibility.

Important SEO strategies include on-page SEO, off-page SEO, technical SEO, and local SEO. Staying on top of the latest SEO trends and Google algorithm changes is also vital.

4.5. Analyzing and Refining

Finally, the only way to continually improve is to measure your results, learn from the data, and refine your strategies. Implement analytics tools like Google Analytics and social media insights to track your progress.

Periodically analyze the data, figure out what's working and what's not, and adjust your strategies accordingly.

4.6. Keeping Up with Digital Marketing Trends

The realm of digital marketing is always evolving. As a digital marketer, you need to stay updated with emerging trends, new technologies, and shifts in consumer behavior to shape your strategies successfully.

4.7. Conveying Value and Trust

Above all, through your digital marketing strategies, you should convey value and trust to your audience. Give them reasons to choose you over competitors. Are you providing high-quality content? Are your products/services top-notch? Are you responsive to queries and complaints?

Your marketing strategies should clearly showcase your value proposition and build your audience's trust.

In conclusion, a robust digital marketing strategy consists of understanding your audience, developing an effective content strategy, utilizing social media, optimizing for search engines, continuously measuring and refining, keeping up with trends, and conveying value and trust. By mastering these elements, you will lay a strong foundation for your digital marketing agency to thrive.

Remember, persistence and adaptability are keys in the digital marketing world. It's not a 'set and forget' game; it's an ongoing process of testing, learning, and improving.

The journey might be challenging, but with the right strategies and mindsets, the rewards can be immensely fulfilling. Start your digital marketing agency with a well-structured method and pave your way towards success.

Chapter 5. Building Your Dream Team

Understanding who your ideal team members are and how to attract them to your agency is crucial to your success. Let's delve into the intricacies of building your dream team.

5.1. Identifying Skills Needed

The first step is identifying the skills your team will need to excel in the realm of digital marketing. You may need content creators, SEO experts, social media managers, web developers, graphic designers, digital advertising professionals, and more. Each of these roles contributes a unique piece to the digital marketing puzzle.

5.2. Hiring the Right Talent

It's essential to find highly skilled professionals who are passionate about their work. Look for candidates with strong portfolios that demonstrate their skills and creativity. But remember, hard skills can be learned. It's their soft skills, like communication, creativity, leadership, problem-solving, and teamwork that can be decisive.

5.3. Building a Maximized Roster

When starting, consider hiring individuals who can fill multiple roles. This strategy maximizes your budget and increases flexibility in project delivery. As your agency grows, you can hire dedicated professionals for each role.

5.4. Remote vs. On-Site Teams

The digital nature of your business means that having a remote team is entirely feasible. Remote work can give you a broader talent pool to hire from, and it can save costs. However, managing a remote team can pose challenges in communication and collaboration. An on-site team, on the other hand, may offer more direct control and easier collaboration, but limits your talent pool to your local area and may incur additional costs.

5.5. Outsourcing Tasks

Consider outsourcing tasks that are not part of your core services, or for skills you don't yet have on your team. This can be a more cost-effective alternative to hiring.

5.6. Retaining Valuable Team Members

Retaining your team is just as important as building it. Fostering a positive work culture, providing growth opportunities, and offering competitive benefits are effective retention strategies.

5.7. Ongoing Team Development

Invest in your staff by providing opportunities for continuous skill development. This not only adds value to your team but also translates into better service for your clients.

5.8. Effective Communication

Open and clear communication is a hallmark of successful teams. Set up regular team meetings, create clear channels of communication, and encourage open dialogue.

5.9. Promoting Leadership

Encourage your team members to take on leadership roles in their areas. This helps foster a sense of ownership and can lead to increased accountability and enthusiasm for work.

5.10. Team Building Activities

Whether you're managing an on-site or remote team, team building activities can enhance a sense of camaraderie, improve communication, and increase productivity.

Building a team may seem daunting, but it's an essential piece of the entrepreneurial journey. With the right mix of skills, culture, and growth, you can assemble a dream team that will pave the way to your digital marketing agency's success.

Chapter 6. Essential Tools for Your Digital Marketing Agency

Every digital marketing agency, regardless of its size or client base, relies on a suite of essential tools. Using the correct blend of tools can significantly enhance your productivity, streamline your workflows, and ultimately, lead to better results for your clients. In this chapter, we delve into a wide array of resources and tools fundamental to running a digital marketing agency successfully.

6.1. SEO and Keyword Analysis Tools

Search Engine Optimization (SEO) and keyword analysis are integral parts of digital marketing. SEO helps boost the visibility of a website on search engines like Google by aligning its content with what potential visitors are searching for.

1. **Google Keyword Planner**: This is a free-as-in-beer tool offered by Google, aimed primarily at advertisers. It provides keyword suggestions, search volumes, and cost per click data, thereby helping you identify high-performing keywords.

2. **SEMrush**: SEMrush is a comprehensive tool offering SEO, PPC, and social media marketing assistance. Some of its standout features include competitive analysis, backlink auditing, and keyword research.

3. **Ahrefs**: Ahrefs is, at its core, a backlink checker but compromises on nothing CRM-related. It provides elaborate reports about backlinks, organic keywords, and rankings.

6.2. Content Creation and Collaboration Tools

Compelling content plays a critical role in attracting and retaining the target audience. It's worth investing in tools that streamline content creation and collaboration process.

1. **Google Docs**: A universally used tool that facilitates real-time collaboration, version control, and editing. With Google Docs, multiple team members can simultaneously work on a document.

2. **Canva**: Canva is user-friendly graphic design software. It incorporates an extensive array of templates, graphics, and images, enabling you to create eye-catching visual content.

3. **Grammarly**: A cloud-based writing assistant that helps avoid grammar and spelling errors, ensuring the high quality of your written content.

6.3. Social Media Management Tools

Social media platforms are instrumental in reaching diverse audience sets. However, managing multiple platforms simultaneously can be overwhelming; tech tools can help.

1. **Hootsuite**: Hootsuite allows you to manage multiple social media accounts from one dashboard. You can create, schedule, and analyze posts across different platforms.

2. **Buffer**: Another popular social media management tool, Buffer excels in its simplicity and user-friendliness. It allows you to schedule posts, manage all your accounts, and get detailed analytics.

6.4. Email Marketing Tools

Email marketing is a time-tested tool for engaging audiences and fostering customer relationships. It's ideal for sharing personalized content, promotional offers, and company news.

1. **MailChimp**: Offering a beginner-friendly email marketing platform, MailChimp lets you design and automate your email campaigns. Its built-in analytics help track the performance of your campaigns.

2. **Constant Contact**: This tool provides a comprehensive set of email advertising tools, including audience segmentation, autoresponders, and survey tools.

3. **SendinBlue**: A cloud-based email marketing tool known for its excellent automation features, enabling you to create, schedule, and monitor campaign performance.

6.5. Marketing Automation Tools

Marketing automation integrates various marketing efforts into a unified strategy, enabling personalized campaigns that resonate more effectively with customers.

1. **HubSpot**: HubSpot does it all—CRM, email marketing, SEO, social media, and analytics. It's an all-in-one platform that helps ensure your marketing efforts are synchronized and impactful.

2. **ActiveCampaign**: Another holistic marketing automation tool combining email marketing, sales, CRM, and messaging features into a single platform for better coordination.

6.6. Analytics Tools

Understanding and analyzing your marketing efforts is vital to make data-driven decisions and improve campaign effectiveness.

1. **Google Analytics**: This is perhaps the most popular digital analytics software. It provides detailed statistics about website traffic, traffic sources, conversions, user behavior, and much more.

2. **BuzzSumo**: This tool is ideal for gauging content performance and gauge audience interests. It shows what content performs best for any topic or competitor.

These are just the "tip of the iceberg" tools to get you started. There's a much larger ecosystem of digital marketing tools available, each with its unique offerings. Be prepared to indulge in some experimentation and fine-tuning to find the combination that works best for your agency. Remember, the essential toolset varies based on your agency size, clientele, and the marketing services you provide.

Chapter 7. Establishing a Strong Online Presence

Your agency's online presence serves as its digital storefront—it's where prospects will discover your services, get a feel for your expertise, and ultimately decide whether they wish to engage with your business. With that in mind, it essential to establish a strong, compelling, and effective online presence that reflects your branding, services, and expertise accurately.

7.1. Creating a Professional Website

The first step in crafting your online presence is creating a professional website—a home for your brand on the internet. Your website should provide concise, clear, and compelling information about your agency and the services you offer.

To start, you'll need a domain name that is relevant, unique, and preferably includes the name of your agency. Ensure your web design is clean, modern, and easy to navigate, with fast load times, as these are factors significantly impacting user experience and even more so— SEO.

Your website's content needs to clearly communicate what you do, why you do it, and who you do it for. It's beneficial to have separate pages for each of your services. Make your site resource-rich by adding a blog that showcases your expertise in the industry. And most importantly, provide multiple, easy-to-find methods for prospects to contact you.

7.2. Utilizing SEO Best Practices

Search engine optimization (SEO) is the practice of optimizing your website to appear higher in search results. By targeting specific keywords that your potential clients may be using, you can help ensure that your website is found by the right people.

Begin your SEO efforts by conducting keyword research using tools like Google Keyword Planner, SEMrush, or Ahrefs. These will help you understand what specific terms your target audience uses when searching for services like yours. Once you have identified these keywords, incorporate them into your site's content, meta descriptions, URLs, and image tags.

Also, remember that off-page SEO, including backlinks, is just as important. Consider writing guest blog posts for other websites in your sector to help build these backlinks while also establishing your authority.

7.3. Embracing Social Media Marketing

Social media platforms offer tremendous value for businesses, providing a powerful way to engage with prospects. Look into platforms like Twitter, LinkedIn, Facebook, Instagram, and YouTube to see where your target audience hangs out. Build a profile that represents your brand well and starts sharing valuable content to engage your audience.

Constant posting of valuable content will grow your followers organically. Interact with your audience by responding to comments and messages in a timely manner. Be sure to share your blog posts on social media to drive traffic back to your website while demonstrating your industry expertise.

Eventually, you might want to look into options for paid social media ads for increased reach.

7.4. Leveraging Email Marketing

Email marketing is one of the most cost-effective ways to communicate with your existing customers and nurture leads. Begin by cultivating an email list—offer an incentive on your website in exchange for an email address, such as a free eBook or consultation. Once you have collected a robust email list, start engaging with subscribers regularly, but don't spam.

Your email communication should provide genuine value to the reader and drive them very gradually towards conversion. Successful email marketing is about building trust and relationships over time.

7.5. Offering High-Quality Content

Content is the queen of digital marketing; it helps drive traffic to your site, engage your audience, and demonstrate your expertise. Plus, high-quality content contributes to SEO efforts.

You should aim to create and publish high-quality blog posts, infographics, and videos that provide insights and answer your audience's questions. Remember: the purpose of your content is to provide value first. Promotion is secondary.

7.6. Collect and Highlight Testimonials

Customer testimonials are a very effective form of social proof—they show prospective customers that you have a solid track record of satisfying clients. Collect testimonials from happy customers, and prominently display them on your website. If possible, include specifics about how your services helped, painting a vivid picture of what you can do for other businesses.

In conclusion, building a strong online presence for your digital marketing agency is about much more than just having a website. It requires a strategic combination of a crisp, professional website, SEO best practices, active social media marketing, targeted email marketing, high-quality content, and effective use of testimonials. Done right, your online presence can become your most powerful marketing tool, helping you appeal to and win over new customers.

Chapter 8. Client Acquisition: Strategies and Tactics

Before diving headfirst into client acquisition tactics, it's crucial to understand that acquiring clients is about building relationships. This is predicated on a good understanding of who your audience is, what they need, how they communicate, and how your services can meet their needs. Once you've established this foundational understanding, you can consider the following strategies and tactics to deepen your client list.

8.1. Identify Your Target Market

The first step in client acquisition is identifying and understanding your target market. This involves conducting exhaustive market research to define your ideal client. Evaluate the type of clients you wish to serve, their industry, size, location, and their overall needs. Understanding these demographics will enable you to form an effective marketing and sales strategy that speaks directly to this audience.

8.2. Develop Your Unique Selling Proposition (USP)

Your USP is what sets you apart from your competitors. It should be compelling enough that prospective clients can quickly visualize the unique value you offer. Consider what your agency excels at, how it compares to your competition, and what makes your service genuinely unique. Once you have a clear USP, incorporate it in all your marketing campaigns.

8.3. Leverage Content Marketing

Content marketing can be a powerful client acquisition tool, especially for a digital marketing agency. Authoritative, helpful content not only establishes your agency as an industry leader but also attracts potential clients who are looking for solutions that your expertise can solve. Invest time in developing relevant blog posts, case studies, eBooks, and webinars that demonstrate your skills and provide value to your audience.

8.4. Employ SEO Strategies

SEO is all about making it easier for potential clients to find your agency online. By optimizing your website and content for specific keywords your potential clients are likely to use, you can improve your site's visibility in search engine rankings. Be sure to stay up-to-date with the latest SEO best practices, as these often change due to algorithm updates.

8.5. Leverage Social Media

Social media isn't just a platform for socializing; it's also an effective client acquisition tool. LinkedIn, in particular, is an excellent platform to connect with business professionals who might require digital marketing services. Build a robust online presence, engage in meaningful conversations, share your recent work and thought leadership content, and advertise your services to reach a broader audience.

8.6. Implement Pay-Per-Click (PPC) Advertising

This digital marketing tactic involves placing ads on search engines like Google or social media platforms and paying a fee each time your ad gets clicked. PPC can help your agency appear at the top of search results, increasing visibility and potentially driving traffic to your website. Remember, to obtain quality leads from PPC, your ads and landing pages must be compelling and optimized for conversion.

8.7. Network at Industry Events

Take advantage of industry events, both online and offline, to meet potential clients. Participate as a speaker or panelist to highlight your expertise, join discussions, or simply attend to network and build relationships. Remember to follow up with the people you connect with, and don't forget to bring along your business cards!

8.8. Use Cold Outreach

While it may be seen as old fashioned or aggressive, cold outreach can still be effective when done correctly. The key is personalization; if you can provide a potential client with a solution to a specific problem they are experiencing, they will be more likely to listen to what you have to say. Remember to be helpful and sell the value of your services rather than being overly promotional.

8.9. Harness the Power of Referrals

Referrals from satisfied customers are some of the best leads you can receive. To encourage referrals, provide exceptional service to all clients and consider implementing a referral program that rewards clients for recommending your services to others.

Taking consistent action on these strategies can lead to a steady stream of new clients. The key is to be patient; it may take time to see results from your client acquisition efforts. Remember, digital marketing is an ever-evolving landscape; stay flexible and be ready to adapt your strategies as needed to maintain success.

Chapter 9. Setting a Pricing Structure: A Balanced Approach

Before we delve into the depths of setting a pricing structure for your digital marketing agency, let's establish a foundational understanding. Pricing in the context of services is a delicate balance between what you believe your services are worth, and what the market is willing to pay. Too high a price and you risk losing prospective clients; too low and you might devalue your services or even struggle to meet operational costs. Understanding how to strike the right balance is crucial to the success of your venture.

9.1. Why Pricing Matters

Successful pricing strategies aren't pulled out of thin air but are the result of careful thought, research, and strategic planning. It supports your agency's financial health, influences how the market perceives your brand, and can directly affect your sales. It's not about setting a price and forgetting it; rather, it's a dynamic part of your business that should be revisited and adjusted as needed.

9.2. Determining the Costs

Your first step in setting a pricing structure is to fully understand your costs. These costs can be broadly classified into two categories: fixed and variable.

Variable Costs: These are dependent on the nature of the work and vary from project to project. Variable costs may include additional employee hours, contracting freelancers, or specific software required for a project.

Add up these costs to determine the baseline of what you need to charge to keep your agency functioning.

9.3. Know Your Value

The next step is to estimate the value that you offer. This is more than just the raw services; it's the solutions and results you provide. Look at the problems you are solving for your clients and the direct benefits they receive. This will help you justify your prices to the client and can also help differentiate your services from competitors.

9.4. Market Research

Market research is key to understanding the going rate for services in your industry. Analyze your competitors not just on a local level, but globally as well. Remember, digital marketing is not geographically bound; you can offer your services anywhere, so it's important to have a broad understanding of market prices. Look at how your potential competitors are pricing their services and the value they claim to provide at that price.

9.5. Pricing Models

There are four primary pricing models in digital marketing: hourly rate, project-based rate, retainer, and value-based pricing.

Value-Based Pricing: This model involves pricing based on the value you provide to your clients. This can be the most lucrative but also the most challenging to implement.

Each model has its own pros and cons, and the one you choose should reflect the nature of your agency. It might also be useful to offer a mix of these to meet different clients' needs.

9.6. Experimentation and Adjustment

Finally, expect to adjust your pricing models as you grow and learn more about your market. Client feedback, market trends, and your financial performance are all good indicators of when it is time to reassess your pricing.

Setting a balanced pricing structure is no small feat, but this foundational knowledge should guide you as you navigate this crucial aspect of your digital marketing agency.

Chapter 10. Scaling Your Digital Marketing Agency

Taking your digital marketing agency from startup to full-fledged business, scaled to handle hundreds if not thousands of clients, is a process that requires foresight, meticulous planning, knowledge of industry trends, innovative strategies, and the sheer tenacity of a focused entrepreneur. Below we delve into what it takes to scale a digital marketing agency to its full potential.

10.1. Getting Your Basics Right

Before even thinking about scaling, it's essential that your agency is set up correctly. This means having a clear business model, a well-defined target audience, a strong value proposition, and unrivaled customer services. You should also have strong relationships with all your stakeholders and a brand that speaks brilliance in the digital marketing landscape.

10.2. Building a Team That Grows With You

Scaling your business means you can't do everything yourself. You'll need to hire a team that embraces your vision and works alongside you, sharing your agency's journey towards growth. Start by identifying what roles need to be filled, then carefully select individuals whose skills and attitudes align with your company culture. Regular training programs should be arranged to sharpen their skills, keeping them up-to-date with the latest digital marketing tools and strategies.

10.3. Financial Management and Asset Optimization

Proper financial management is critical when scaling your agency. This includes tracking expenses, optimizing costs, ensuring consistent cash flow, and securing adequate funds for investment in growth. Effective asset optimization involves the best use of your agency's assets, whether they are physical, digital, or human resources.

10.4. Diversifying Your Services

As you scale your agency, offering a wider range of services may help attract a broader clientele, thus boosting your revenue streams. Possible service diversifications include SEO, content marketing, social media marketing, email marketing, website design and development, analytics, PPC campaigns, and so on.

10.5. Refining Your Marketing Funnel

Your marketing funnel serves as your client acquisition tool. In a scaled business model, it's essential to automate this process as much as possible. With the help of cutting-edge CRM tools, you can automate email sequences, track leads, analyze metrics, and engage with clients on various platforms, all in real-time.

10.6. Building Strong Client Relationships

The strength of your client relationships directly contributes to the success of your agency and its ability to scale. Happy clients act as brand ambassadors, spreading word about your services, resulting in brand credibility and trust, thus attracting more clients.

10.7. Leveraging Technology for Growth

Harnessing the power of technology is key to scale your digital marketing operations. Using tools like SEO optimizers, analytics platforms, ad management systems, project management software, and more, can take care of repetitive tasks, provide insightful data and allow your team to focus on what they do best - being creative.

10.8. Partnerships and Collaborations

Forming strategic partnerships can provide your agency with a competitive edge, providing the potential for accessing new markets, sharing resources, and co-creating innovative campaigns. It might be timely to explore tie-ups with ad networks, marketing platforms, or even other marketing agencies.

Scaling a digital marketing agency can be a rewarding journey. It requires a deep understanding of your agency, continuous learning and adaptation, strong financial management, and a dedicated team. Remember, the scale of your agency doesn't just reflect in the number of your employees or revenue. It also shines through the reputation and credibility that your agency has in the marketplace. Be patient, stay dedicated, adapt and execute, and watch your digital marketing agency thrive.

Chapter 11. Maintaining Industry Relevance: Trends, Innovations and More

The digital marketing landscape is a tumultuous sea of constant change, awash with countless trends and innovations that continue to redefine the industry's status quo. A digital marketing agency that fails to stay relevant risks being swept away by the tide of progress. Hence, maintaining industry relevance is not a luxury but a survival necessity. This chapter illuminates the path towards industry relevance by unraveling key trends, showcasing innovative practices, and more.

11.1. Understanding the Importance of Relevance

Before diving into the ocean of trends and innovations, it's essential to comprehend why relevance is critical in digital marketing. Firstly, clients seek agencies that are aware of the latest strategies and technologies that can help them outperform their competitors. The ability to offer the latest, most effective solutions can make or break client relationships. Secondly, as an agency, staying up-to-date is vital to attract and retain talent, demonstrating that your agency is at the industry's cutting edge.

11.2. Spotting Trends: The Art and Science

Identifying emerging trends in digital marketing can seem intimidating. With endless streams of news, case studies, blogs, and social media chatter, it's sometimes challenging to separate the wheat from the chaff. However, trendspotting is both an art and a science, merging analytical data investigation with creative intuition. Following credible industry publications, attending webinars and conferences, and tracking key performance indicators can arm you with the knowledge required to anticipate new trends.

11.3. Top Current Digital Marketing Trends

The digital marketing sphere is alive with innovation. A plethora of trends are unfolding and will continue to impact the industry in various ways, ranging from ever-evolving social media platforms to advancing artificial intelligence (AI) technologies. By taking note of these emerging trends, you can strategize to stay ahead of your competition.

1. Social Media - New platforms continue to rise, such as the rapid ascent of TikTok, while Instagram and Facebook continue to release new features. Be sure your team is prepared to adapt to these changes, leverage the unique opportunities they present, and craft strategies aligned with each platform's nuances.

2. Content Marketing - Blogs and articles remain important, but the proliferation of formats like video, podcasts, and interactive content are reshaping the landscape. Tapping into these burgeoning formats can help diversify your offerings and appeal to a wider audience.

3. Personalization - With the deluge of digital content, mass marketing is proving less effective. Personalization, fueled by AI and big data, allows for highly targeted, individual-centric marketing, enhancing engagement rates, and boosting conversions.

11.4. The Role of Technology and Innovation

There is no denying the disruptive influence of technology on digital marketing. From the rise of AI and machine learning to the advancement in data analytics, new tools and technologies are continually unfurling, pushing the boundaries of what's possible in digital marketing.

1. AI-Driven Marketing - Leveraging AI can help automate routine tasks, deliver personalized content and advertisements, and provide insights into customer behavior. Embracing AI should be a priority for agencies that wish to stay relevant.

2. Voice Search - With the proliferation of smart speakers and virtual assistants, voice search is growing exponentially. Optimizing for voice search should be a key consideration in your SEO strategy.

3. Chatbots - As customer experience increasingly becomes a differentiator, chatbots present a way to provide instant, personalized customer service. Incorporating chatbots can help elevate your client's customer experience and drive brand loyalty.

11.5. The Importance of Continuous Learning

The only constant in digital marketing is change. Thus, constant learning is vitrarily for any agency wishing to maintain industry relevance. This can include formal training, attending seminars and webinars, or even informal methods like following industry thought leaders and networking.

11.6. Conclusion: Don't Just Survive, Thrive

Maintaining industry relevance is a balancing act between adapting to trends and leveraging technology alongside fostering a culture of continuous learning. By giving due attention to these elements, your agency won't just survive the digital marketing storm; it will thrive amidst the chaos, making waves of its own.

Carve out your path in the dynamic world of digital marketing by staying alert, adaptable, and invested in the latest movements shaping the landscape. As you traverse through the thrilling yet challenging voyage of discovering, assimilating, and implementing trends and innovations, remember - the journey is as rewarding as the destination.